TRANSGENDER LIVES

Twenty-First Century Books
A division of Lerner Publishing Group, Inc.
241 First Avenue North
Minneapolis, MN 55401 U.S.A.

For reading levels and more information, look up this title at
www.lernerbooks.com.

Main body text set in Perpetua MT Std 12/15.
Typeface provided by Monotype Typography.

Library of Congress Cataloging-in-Publication Data

Cronn-Mills, Kirstin, 1968-
    Transgender lives/ by Kirstin Cronn-Mills.
        pages   cm
    Includes bibliographical references and index.
    ISBN 978–0–7613–9022–0 (lib. bdg. : alk. paper)
    ISBN 978–1–4677–4796–7 (eBook)
    1. Transgender people—United States—Juvenile literature.
  2. Transsexuals—United States—Juvenile literature.
  3. Transsexualism—United States—Juvenile literature.
  I. Title.
  HQ77.95.U6.C76 2015
  306.76'8—dc23   2013022604

Manufactured in the United States of America
1 – PC – 7/15/14

TRANSGENDER LIVES

COMPLEX STORIES, COMPLEX VOICES

KIRSTIN CRONN-MILLS

TWENTY-FIRST CENTURY BOOKS * MINNEAPOLIS

AUTHOR'S NOTE

As a cisgender individual, I have done my utmost to accurately represent the many facets of transgender experience contained in this book—but I am no expert. The experts on transgender lives are the individuals who live those lives every day, from birth to death, within this book and in our world.

Enormous thanks and appreciation go to Nancy Bebernes, Katie Burgess, Dave Gaer, Julia Keleher, Dean Kotula, Hayden Northup (his sister Karlee; his mom, Diana; and his fiancée, Adriana), Natasha Rosenberg, and Brooke Wilcoxson for agreeing to be a part of this book. They are wonderful human beings and kind friends, and I have learned enormously from them.

Deep debts of gratitude go to Alex Jackson Nelson and James DeWitt for their thorough and interrogative reads of this manuscript, and I send many thanks to Libby Stille for her research assistance. Special thanks and much appreciation go to Domenica Di Piazza for the opportunity to write this book and for being such an insightful editor.

CONTENTS

INTRODUCTION

Awesome! It's the day you get to apply for a driver's license. As you fill out the form, you realize you have to choose between the boxes labeled "male" and "female." But what do you do if you feel neither box fits you? Today you're dressed like a guy. Tomorrow you might wear a skirt. The doctor gave you a label at birth, based on what your body looked like, but sometimes that label doesn't fit. Sometimes you identify with both boxes, some days with neither, and someday you might transition from one gender to another. But what to do now? Do you make a new box? Do you lie? You compromise by checking the one that seems closest to who you are—at least for today.

* * *

Does this story seem strange to you? Are you thinking, "What the heck do you mean? Of course I know which box to check!" For many of us, our gender identity is very straightforward. If the doctor determined that your body was female when you were born and if your brain tells you to act as other women do, then you're a woman. Easy, right? For some people, their brain's messages (gender) match up with their body (sex). But for other people, gender identity is much more complex. Some individuals' brains tell them they're one gender, but their body tells them something else. Some people feel like several genders at once, while some people feel they're in between genders. Some individuals feel like no gender at all.

TRANS*PERSPECTIVE: TRANS*PUNCTUATION

In the Internet world, placing an asterisk (*) after a search term indicates you are looking for any and all information related to the search term. Including an asterisk after the word *trans** is a way to include all individuals who identify in some way with a "trans" identity.

For the individuals in this book, being a trans* person is only one part of who each person is. The people in this book are partners, siblings, and someone's children. They have jobs, hobbies, favorite TV shows, and foods they hate, just like any other individual you know.

The trans* world, its terms, and its ideas will continue to shift and grow over time. Each individual who is trans* will define their life and their identity in different ways. For this reason, this book is only an introduction to, not an exhaustive exploration of, life within the transgender spectrum.

CHAPTER ONE

HAYDEN, KARLEE, DIANA, AND ADRIANA

My first memory I have that has any significance to my current lifestyle was when I was in preschool. It was potty-break time. We lined up, boys in one line, girls in the other. Yep, you guessed it, I lined up with the boys. I remember getting yanked to the other line with the girls. I didn't really pay much attention to it, but for some reason that memory has stayed with me. I think I always knew who I was, but society made me feel like my feelings couldn't be validated in real life. So, I did my best. I tucked all of my feelings inside.

—Hayden

Hayden *(left)* loves football, hunting, fishing, and hanging out with family. He is in his early twenties, is in college, has three siblings, and lives in a small town in the Midwest. Hayden grew up as Haylee, and when he realized he couldn't live any longer as a female, he moved four hours away from his hometown. He cut his long hair and stopped communicating with his family—but only for a while. Once he sorted out what he needed to do, he sent his mom a photo of his short hairstyle. When she responded, Hayden told her about his need to transition from female to male, and that short conversation changed his world forever.

Not long after the encouraging exchange with his mother, Hayden moved back home and began his physical transition from female to male.

As the first step, he began to give himself prescribed injections of testosterone (the hormone that creates male body characteristics). Over time, he saw himself become more masculine. His voice deepened, and he gained muscle mass very quickly. Fearful of facing disrespectful reactions, he kept himself as safe as he could from other people. Hayden remembers, "I sort of stayed in hiding until my voice started to change; I was protecting myself from hateful people. I was like a hibernating bear, waiting for the weather to change, and then I would climb out of my cave and explore the world again."

Even at the beginning of his journey, Hayden had many loyal people supporting him. For example, his former softball coach reached out to him when she learned of Hayden's transition. "She told me how proud she was of me and that she . . . had my back. Coach said, 'You are so brave to go through this in such a narrow-minded town.' I printed [her] e-mail and keep it in my wallet. I take it out whenever I'm feeling down."

KARLEE, HAYDEN'S SISTER

Hayden's family has been his main support throughout his transition. But it's his sister Karlee, five years older than Hayden, who's been his rock. She sensed things weren't comfortable for Hayden very early in Hayden's life. Hayden and Karlee's mom liked them to wear "girly" clothes sometimes, and that was fine with Karlee. But Hayden had reservations. Speaking about Hayden when he was still Haylee, Karlee remembers:

> One day, the neighbor lady, whose son was Hayden's best friend, came to my mom with concern on why her seven-year-old son had a bunch of my mom's six-year-old daughter's white, lacy socks hiding under his bed. I think she thought there was something wrong with her son, foot fetish, maybe? But Hayden confessed that he was paying the neighbor boy with leftover Easter/Halloween/Christmas candy to hide them from my mom. Hayden was determined to not wear the "girly" lace socks.

After that, Karlee noticed other ways that Hayden wasn't a traditional sister, from the way he dressed to the things he did with his friends. When Hayden was in high school, Karlee had even more confirmation that Hayden wasn't comfortable as Haylee. Karlee says:

> One day, during a family gathering, I brought up prom and asked him if he was going to go, and if so what kind of dress was he going to wear, and if I could please, please, do his hair for the event. I wanted to do something special like that for him. But as I talked about it, he appeared to become more and more agitated with me. I could tell that he wanted me to stop talking about it, but I didn't. It was a milestone that I wanted to be a part of and help him with his hair and makeup to make him look the most beautiful out of any girl there. I could see that I'd started a very uncomfortable conversation and realized that I'd better stop it. Hayden became very quiet. He looked so sad. I felt so wrong for making him uncomfortable.

Karlee was able to put the puzzle pieces together a few years later, when Hayden told her about his impending transition. She knew Hayden was becoming the person he needed to be. Karlee says, "To me, Hayden has always been Haylee. He is the same person, [who] just has a different name now. I feel like I cannot compare Hayden to ever being a sister. He always felt more like a brother than a sister to me."

DIANA, HAYDEN'S MOM

Hayden's mom knew something was different about Hayden early in his life. She remembers:

> I felt I was raising a boy, [who was] growing into a man . . . without the correct gender. I [only] *felt* those words at the time, [but] I [know how to express] it now. I remember saying to my

[own] mom when Haylee was little, "She is a real tomboy." Then, as he got older, I would tell my mom, "I have this knowing she is not gay, but *what* [she is] I just can't figure it out." I said those very words many times. My mom felt the same, [and so did] Hayden's two sisters and brother.

Hayden's transition was very emotional for Diana. She knew she had to support him through everything, but she felt sadness about losing a daughter. And it was very hard for Diana to discover the pain Hayden had been in for so long:

I believe I went through all the stages of [grief] in the beginning of [Hayden's] transition. I wanted to hold on to Haylee, [and my] parenting skills stayed the same, but I was lost, weak from loss, and so shockingly mad that my baby had to suffer through the years and I wasn't aware of his pain. Although Hayden was experiencing [the] transition, I found myself [reacting as] a fighter, holding him up. I am his mom, and I communicated with [him for] hours and hours [to build] strength in him . . . [but] I cried endlessly for him and for me once I hung up the phone or walked away.

At the same time, Diana knows Hayden did what he needed to do. She says, "I am so proud of my son! He has given me the opportunity to grow in ways I could never dream [of]. He is my blessing."

HAYDEN'S LIFE NOW

Before Hayden legally changed his name and gender, some encounters were very confusing. Hayden recalls that "the absolute worst part of all would be when I would apply for a job. Once, I had an awesome job lined up, and right after they said I got the job, they changed their mind after seeing my ID card. So then I was afraid to apply anywhere." All of that shifted when Hayden went before a judge and presented his petition to legally change his name and switch his gender marker from F to M. Now that Hayden is legally male, he has no problem with applying for jobs or filling out official forms.

Hayden's physical transition is also complete, and nobody would mistake him for a woman. Hayden had a double mastectomy (also referred to as "top" surgery) so his chest would be more like a male chest. He says his top surgery made him the happiest he's ever been in his life.

TRANS*PERSPECTIVE: THE *T* IN LGBT

In general, when people write or speak about the lesbian, gay, bisexual, and transgender community, they use some version of the acronym LGBT to refer to individuals who belong to this community. This acronym can also be written LBTG or GLBT. You may also see a *Q* as part of the acronym, standing for "queer," a more flexible way to classify sexual orientation. To be all-inclusive, the acronym is sometimes LGBTQQIA— lesbian, gay, bisexual, transgender, queer, questioning (not sure of one's sexual orientation), intersex, and ally (a supporter of the community).

Some individuals question why the *T* is part of this commonly used acronym. If you refer to someone as lesbian, gay, or bisexual (LGB), you are referring to a person's sexual orientation. But the *T* relates to gender identity, not to sexual identity, and trans* individuals have many different sexual orientations. For that reason, some trans* individuals wish to remove the *T* from the LGBT acronym because it relates to a completely different type of identity.

Hayden is now public about his transition and speaks to groups of people about his life. Hayden also says he's had to grow up fast in order to take care of himself and to work on his transition, but all the hassle is worth the time and effort he puts into it. His new fiancée, Adriana, says this about their relationship:

> When I first met Hayden, I already knew of his identity of being a "Trans Man". At the time, we were just friends of a mutual friend. I didn't think much about it because he and I were both in relationships at that time. . . . When Hayden and I started dating, we never really talked . . . [because] it wasn't an issue for me. I knew he wanted to have that conversation, just to get the elephant out of the room! So, we did. He talked about his inability to help have children and his current name and gender marker, and how it would affect our chances of getting married as heterosexuals. He also explained the daily challenges he faces emotionally and physically.
>
> All of his worries were definitely valid, but, they didn't bother me. I guess my feelings for him overcame the future struggles we would face together. I didn't and haven't looked at Hayden in any way other than a biological male. His [status as a trans* man] never gets brought up in conversation unless it is about his name change or possible surgeries he may want. Otherwise, our relationship is the same as any other couple. Sure, we will have to face future challenges when we try to have children, but many couples have those same challenges.

Right now, Hayden is in school, focusing on becoming a paramedic and a teacher. Together, Hayden and Adriana are working on saving money and taking care of all the details that come with creating a new life. They're planning their wedding and enjoying themselves. Hayden says he's proud of himself and all he's done, and for the first time in his life, he's happy.

CHAPTER TWO

TRANS*GENDER BASICS

Sex is a biological concept. When we are born, doctors look at our bodies and our genitals and label our sex based on what they see. A person's biological sex comes from genes and primary and secondary sex characteristics (genitals, internal reproductive organs, hair growth patterns, muscle mass, and other physical factors). The words *male* and *female* represent the sexes of most human beings.

Gender identity, on the other hand, is an internal sense that is assisted by the society around us. Our gender identity comes from our brains, not our bodies, and is heavily influenced by how the society in which we live defines gender. Traditionally, societies view gender as a binary, having only two options—man or woman, masculine or feminine. The socially constructed gender binary creates gender roles, which are sets of behaviors that a society says are appropriate for men and women. For example, in many societies, the gender role for women is to stay home to care for children, while the gender role for men is to work outside the home.

If an individual's gender identity matches that person's biological anatomy, that person is said to be cisgender. The term *cisgender* comes from the Latin prefix *cis*, which means "on the same side." For example, if an individual's body was assigned female at birth and if the individual prefers a traditionally feminine appearance and behavior pattern, the individual is cisgender.

Individuals who are transgender (trans* individuals) are people who have gender identities that do not align with the biology of the sex assigned to them. In fact, the Latin prefix *trans* means "across," "beyond," "through," or "changing thoroughly."

A person's gender identity is that person's sense of being male or female or both or neither. Gender identity can be flexible throughout our lifetimes. Most people become aware of what they view as their true gender identity in childhood. An individual's gender presentation (or gender expression) is the way in which that person chooses to represent their gender identity to the world, regardless of that person's biological sex. Gender can be

TRANS*PERSPECTIVE: PRONOUNS

Pronouns are easy, right? Females use *she* and *her*, and males use *he* and *his*. Not so fast—pronouns are often challenging for many trans* individuals. Sometimes traditionally gendered pronouns just don't fit particular gender identities.

A trans* person might be assigned male at birth but prefer female pronouns. Or a trans* person might prefer *they* and *their* if they don't feel comfortable with either set of gendered pronouns. The English language has also evolved to create gender-neutral pronouns such as *zhe* and *hir*. Some trans* individuals prefer these pronouns.

One of the most affirming and supportive things a cisgender person can do is to ask a trans* person what pronouns fit their gender identity, and then use those pronouns consistently when talking about or referring to them.

expressed through clothing choices, possessions, physical actions, and the kinds of jobs a person chooses, among other things.

A person's gender presentation may or may not match a person's sense of gender identity. For example, in most cases, a feminine-identified person will dress in ways her society views as acceptably and traditionally feminine. Some feminine-identified people, on the other hand, may have bodies that were labeled male when they were born, though they may still prefer to dress and live as women. In other cases, a woman with a biologically female body may feel more comfortable wearing men's clothing. Such nontraditional gender presentation is sometimes referred to as gender variance, gender play, or an atypical gender.

Individuals who are gender-nonconforming may choose many different ways to express themselves. A person's gender presentation may change from masculine to feminine from day to day, or it may rest somewhere between masculine and feminine. Individuals who choose to explore and be flexible about their gender are sometimes said to be gender-bending.

CHAPTER THREE

KATIE BURGESS

*In my life, there was no language around gender. I certainly
vocalized feelings about gender and acted on them plenty,
but I wasn't able to identify as trans* because I didn't know
the word. When I was fourteen, my parents' insurance was
running out, and they sent me to a few therapy appointments.
I went there saying, "I think I'm a girl. Am I crazy?" The
therapist said, "Yeah, absolutely," and I said, "Oh, thank God,
I'm crazy, we can work with that." That was a much better
idea than being transgender.*

—Katie

Katie Burgess is an activist and a street artist in her early thirties. For her
day job, she runs a nonprofit organization that supports trans* youth, and
when she's not doing that, she organizes community gatherings and political
projects. She lives a multifaceted life. She juggles and acts in theater projects,
and she also plays the spoons. She's also been known to skateboard, go to
metal/punk shows, and occasionally hop trains. Currently, she lives in a
large midwestern metropolitan area in a communal family group with two
other adults and their three children.

GROWING UP

When Katie was younger and growing up in New England, she didn't follow
any particular gender script. She notes, "I certainly tried to play with my
neighbors' Barbie dolls, but I also played Teenage Mutant Ninja Turtles

with my brother. Gender wasn't talked about. We were in a small school, and things were relatively fluid with gender." Katie says she comes from a gender-flexible family where she did not experience pressure to conform to gender expectations. Her mother is a bodybuilder, her uncle is trans*, and her brother expresses flexible gender and sexual identities.

Katie came out as a gay man when she was fourteen or fifteen, and she "clung to that word [*gay*] because I knew what it meant." When she was able to move to an urban center and connect with LGBT groups there, she developed a political awareness of what it meant to be part of the LGBT community. But Katie says:

> I didn't hear the word *transgender* until I was eighteen, when a person I was dating came out as trans*. My boyfriend came out as my girlfriend, and I thought, "What the hell is that?" She explained it, thankfully in an intelligent way, with no rigid boundaries. She said, "I just don't think I'm a man." And I said, "Guess what? Neither do I." And then the skies parted, and I understood who I was.

VENTURING OUT

Katie had a hard time accepting her trans* identity at first, and she didn't have any money to start her physical transition. Her life took some dramatic turns. At various times, she and her brother lived in a station wagon, in a tent, on the streets, and in an old bus she called the Happy Food Bus. To earn money, she was involved in both the sex and drug trades. But, she says, "I've always been pretty out. Even on the streets I went by Katie. If anybody asked why, I would tell them I was transgender, and if they didn't believe me, I would go on with my day." Katie and her brother supported each other emotionally during this very crucial time: She says, "We saved each other." Katie also turned to good friends for support during this part of her life, and she feels blessed to count them as family. For Katie, they are "the family you make."

Eventually Katie had enough money to begin her physical transition. The first step was to take hormones. At first, she was a little nervous, but a few years after she started taking estrogen, she had an orchiectomy (removal of her testes), which was a huge relief. As she notes, "Having the orchiectomy meant that I would never again have to face the chemical imbalance of too much testosterone in my body. This imbalance [which can reverse the effects of estrogen] was worse than any other [problem] I had. Even if the apocalypse happened and I couldn't get estrogen, the risks of surgery [pain, infection, long recovery] were worth it to me to be rid of that imbalance."

LIVING NOW

Katie has lived in lots of places in the United States, and she says that transphobia (fear of and discrimination against transgender people) and misogyny (hatred of and discrimination against women) "shift depending on where you are and the culture you're in." She says she stopped moving and settled in her current city because it's very friendly to trans* individuals. "I [feel] welcome, and there [is] a culture of resources [for trans* people] and a way to distribute them. In the San Francisco Bay area, for example, there are far more resources, but the ways the community deals with distributing those resources are very different, because the community is much larger. If you're trans* there, you're not unique, so people assume you'll figure it out [on your own], which doesn't always happen. Here, people say 'talk to X, Y, and Z,' and that's much more helpful."

When asked about her trans* identity, Katie says:

I love all of it. The wisdom I've gleaned from being trans* is who I am. I can't imagine what my life would be like otherwise. [If I hadn't asked all those questions] I would have grown up and not questioned as much as I did in my life, and I'd be a computer programmer and living in Southern Maine. I got to walk a very difficult but very worthwhile path that has really led to a deeper wisdom about myself and a deeper spiritual connection with others, plus more resources, more community, more artistic outlets, and a deeper connection with my body. It's easy for me to talk about the ways [living in] my body has been traumatic, but I've also gotten to question my body in a way lots of people never get to. I've gotten to question my physical and sexual self in ways other people don't, and that's a blessing.

TRANS*PERSPECTIVE: TRANS*LIVES AND MONEY

Money is a complicated topic for everyone, and access (or lack of access) to money can change a trans* person's life in profound ways. For example, sometimes a person has a diagnosis of gender dysphoria (a mismatch between physical anatomy and gender identity) with a treatment plan to have gender reassignment surgery. But if insurance won't cover the surgery and the person can't pay for the surgery, the person is denied medically necessary and life-changing treatment. Or if a trans* individual can't pay for the hormones they need or for a name change they need, their life can be put on hold. If a trans* person loses their job because of their gender presentation, their life may be threatened by poverty, homelessness, and fear.

Whether she's working as an activist or performing her art, Katie is also excited to be *who* she is:

As an artist who practices physical theater, juggling, and dancing, I need that deeper relationship with my body and that ability to ask hard questions when it comes to my relationship with my body, because I'm using my body to make art. Being trans* has brought me to fascinating places—it's a great way to see the world.

CHAPTER FOUR

TRANS*SPECTRUM IDENTITIES

Many different individuals fall under what experts call the trans* spectrum, or the trans* umbrella. "I'm trans*" and "I'm transgender" are ways these individuals might refer to themselves. But there are distinctions among different trans* identities.

Gender-fluid individuals prefer to remain flexible about their gender(s). Some dress in ways that reflect both genders at the same time, while others may express one gender on one day and another gender on another day. Some gender-fluid people choose to express a gender that lies between a masculine and feminine presentation. Terms for individuals who have flexible gender identities may include genderqueer, gender fluid, bigender, transmasculine, transfeminine, neutrois, third gender, trigender, intergender, or androgyne. Androgynous individuals may not identify with either side of the gender binary. Other individuals consider themselves agender, and they may feel they have no gender at all.

Individuals who cross-dress are also part of the trans* spectrum. In the past, cross-dressers were called transvestites, but that term is now considered rude. Some researchers theorize that the term *cross-dresser* may also be passing out of use because individuals who cross-dress are increasingly perceived as genderqueer. People choose to cross-dress for many different reasons, including comfort, sexual pleasure, and public performance. Drag kings and drag queens are performers who use clothing, makeup, hairstyles, and behaviors to appear to be the opposite gender. Being "in drag" is a way to play with gender.

Sometimes intersex individuals are also considered part of the trans* spectrum. People who are intersex are born with a combination of male and female internal and external genitalia. Some individuals may also have a combination of male and female chromosomes other than XX (female) or XY (male). Sometimes the intersex individual, their family, and their doctors choose medical intervention to align the internal and external sexual organs. In the past, medical professionals would make their own determination about a person's gender and perform genital operations shortly after birth to make anatomical changes. Now, doctors strive to involve the intersex individual in the decision and work to understand a person's gender identity before modifying an individual's body.

In the past, intersex individuals were called hermaphrodites, but that term is no longer considered appropriate. In addition, many intersex individuals do not identify as trans* because they have a consistent gender identity. It is only the sex of the internal and external sex organs that do not match each other.

GENDER IDENTITY AND MEDICAL INTERVENTION

The term *transsexual* refers to people whose gender identity does not match the sex assigned to them at birth. Many transsexual individuals decide to use medical intervention, usually hormones and/or surgery, to alter their bodies to match what they feel is their true gender identity. These medical options can be very expensive, and insurance often does not cover the procedures. For these reasons, not all transsexual individuals can afford these procedures.

Usually transsexual individuals are prescribed hormones first, and then they make decisions about what surgeries they will have. Choices about hormones and surgery are usually made in consultation with medical personnel, including endocrinologists, surgeons, and psychologists.

Timelines for receiving hormones and surgeries can vary with the individual needs of each person and with the requirements of each doctor.

If individuals decide to alter their bodies with surgery, they usually choose from the following surgical procedures, depending on what they need and want. For individuals assigned female at birth who are transitioning to a masculine identity, there are several surgical options:

- Oophorectomy (ovary removal) and hysterectomy (uterus removal)
- Mastectomy (breast removal)
- Phalloplasty (creation of a penis and extension of the urethra from skin grafted from other parts of the body)

For individuals assigned male at birth who are transitioning to a feminine identity, there are different surgical and procedural options:

- Facial feminization, including shaving of the Adam's apple
- Full-body hair removal
- Orchiectomy (testes removal)
- Vaginoplasty (inversion of the penis into a vagina)

TRANS*PERSPECTIVE: MICHELLE KOSILEK

In 1990 Michelle Lynne Kosilek, formerly known as Robert John Kosilek, was convicted of murdering her wife, Cheryl McCaul. Kosilek, who had begun transitioning by the time of the murder, has been serving a life sentence without parole in a medium-security men's prison in Norfolk, Massachusetts.

For more than twenty years, Kosilek has been suing the State of Massachusetts for the right to gender reassignment surgery. Kosilek has dressed and lived as a woman while serving her prison time. The state has provided psychotherapy and hormone treatment. Kosilek and her legal team have claimed that surgery is the most appropriate treatment for her gender dysphoria. Because of her medical distress, Kosilek has tried to commit suicide twice and has also tried to castrate herself.

In January 2014, the US Court of Appeals for the First Circuit in Boston backed a lower court's earlier decision that surgery is necessary for Kosilek. The appeals court ruled that state officials had violated Kosilek's constitutional rights by failing to provide the surgery. This decision paves the way for what may become the first court-ordered and state-funded gender confirmation surgery for a prisoner in the United States. It remains to be seen how and when the state's Department of Correction will respond to the decision and how the decision might impact similar cases in other prisons around the country.

CHAPTER FIVE

DEAN KOTULA

What advice would I give a young transsexual person? Instincts told you who you are. You listened, trusted your instincts, and had the courage to go on to realize your true identity. Don't let your transition be your only bold endeavor; use those same abilities again and again throughout your life to fulfill each and every dream you can imagine.

—Dean

Dean Kotula was born in the Midwest and now lives in New England. He is a writer, an antiques dealer, and a fine art and documentary photographer who owns a commercial gallery. He has lived in many different places throughout the world and says he's "not only straddling genders, but centuries. I feel as though I'm [living] in contemporary culture with a nineteenth-century sensibility."

EARLY LIFE

Early in his life, Dean felt different. "I began defining myself by taking charge of what I wore. By age six or so, I refused dresses and skirts and demanded to choose my own clothes. I lucked out in that I was the first kid in the family who didn't have to attend parochial [religious] school; that meant I didn't have to wear a sex-specific uniform." Dean was one of seven siblings and "began to isolate and feel lonely because I began realizing I was different and this difference made others uncomfortable."

Dean also discovered that his childhood crushes on other girls were different from his siblings' love interest in kids of the opposite sex:

I remember discovering my attraction for girls when I got on the bus for the first day of kindergarten. There was a girl seated across the aisle from me who had bangs across her forehead and shoes the color of butterscotch. I decided she was from Holland, and I was in love. Even at that age, spoken or not, I knew there were boundaries I couldn't begin to cross, but I also knew I could feign childhood innocence while walking home with her hand in mine.

When Dean was a teenager, his family returned to the Midwest after living in Hawaii and Thailand for some time. Dean's experiences in both places had an enormous impact on him. He began to think with a broader, more global perspective. This viewpoint clashed with the narrower worldview of his hometown peers. And then there was a matter of adjusting to sexual feelings at a time when same-sex attraction was viewed as wrong. Dean says:

I hated the changes to my body and the implications behind those changes. And I hated having to suppress the sexual attraction I felt towards some of my girlfriends. I never said a word to them about how I felt. Overnights (yes, there were overnights, since we were both considered girls, after all) proved torturous; lying beside someone I was intensely attracted to and not being able to act on it. Listening to girlfriends talk about boys they liked supplied [plenty of] mental torture. I hated myself and my circumstance.

Dean's father was the mayor of the small town where the family lived. For this reason, Dean felt pressure to hide who he was so he wouldn't call attention to himself or his family. Dean knew he was male, but suppressing his male identity had consequences. Dean says, "I didn't know where to turn, so I turned to drugs, ingesting handfuls of hallucinogens and amphetamines on a daily basis. Before long I was in a drug treatment center, where I stayed for nearly eight months. In the end, I went to an alternative high school and received my GED . . . [and went to college] some years later."

TRANSITION

Dean didn't find workable resources to help him make his transition to male until he was thirty-eight years old:

> I visited a gender identity program at the University of Minnesota when I was in my early twenties. They could have helped me and a far greater percentage of transsexuals if they hadn't charged exorbitant fees for their services. They had a long, drawn-out evaluation process, and I couldn't afford their services. I moved, and finally, fifteen years later, connected with a psychiatrist in Portland, Oregon, who had a lot of experience evaluating transsexuals. I was a classic female-to-male (FTM) transsexual. He recognized the signs and wrote out a prescription for hormones during my second, one-hour session with him.

Once Dean began his transition, reactions from family were mixed. One sister declared "I can't relate" and walked away. Dean was hurt and angry. He said to her, "Of course you can't relate; I didn't expect you to understand. I can't relate to space travel, but it doesn't mean I can't show some interest in it, particularly if a brother of mine is heading to the moon!" Another sister was very understanding. "We shared a bedroom growing up, so she saw, more than anyone else, the pain I was suffering. Talking [to her] about my need to transition finally explained some of my puzzling behavior."

MAKING HISTORY

In Oregon, Dean faced on-the-job discrimination related to his gender identity. He tells the story with pride of how he helped bring about historic legal workplace protections for transsexuals.

> I was hired on as one of two female shipyard machinists just prior to receiving my long-awaited prescription for testosterone. I said nothing to my employer regarding my transsexual status or intention

to transition. But a short time after introducing testosterone to my system, the physical changes were apparent. Around that time, I was featured prominently in a national pop-culture magazine. The son of one of the shipyard electricians saw the article and gave it to his dad, who passed it around among the two-thousand-plus employees working in the yard. So, the company saw the changes in me and read the explanation—the whys and wherefores—in the magazine, but no way did they accept it (there were a few exceptions).

I began to be harassed in both subtle and obvious ways. [During work slowdowns], I was usually one of the first to be laid off and one of the last to be called back to work. During one layoff, I called the company and asked the secretary to send me a copy of my work record. Handwritten in the record were the words "was F[emale], now M[ale]. When?" along with a notation stating that I should not be called back. Since I was a union employee, they had to begin to falsify a record of poor performance on my part, or some such thing, in order to justify a dismissal. When I saw the layoff notation linked to their knowledge of my transition (was F, now M) I felt that was proof positive of their decision to discriminate, so I filed a lawsuit against them.

The Bureau of Labor and Industry in Portland, Oregon, investigated and found a positive finding of discrimination against me. I was the first transsexual in the state of Oregon to have a case with a positive finding of discrimination, and my case was instrumental towards gaining statewide protection for transsexuals in the state of Oregon.

FULFILLING HIS DREAMS

A gifted photographer, Dean processed his first photographic images in his father's darkroom when he was ten years old. Today he owns a gallery where he exhibits more than three decades' worth of his photos. He is currently working on a book and has recently won local and national awards for his photography. Dean also owns and works in an antiques shop that caters to summer tourists. Sometimes Dean thinks about running for local office, but "in the same moment I decide against being in the public eye as a token transsexual." His life is peaceful. His partner, Diane, lives in another state, where she runs a psychotherapy practice, and they see each other often. His gallery and antiques business overlook the ocean and a working harbor, which fondly remind him of his days as a commercial fisherman on a shrimp boat in Oregon. Dean says he has learned to love himself and to appreciate the elements of his complex journey. When asked about his identity, he says,

> What do I love about the transsexual part of my identity? Knowing I am far more complex than most people would ever suspect. (I'm sure that I'm generally perceived as just being some boring, middle-aged white guy.) My own experience always reminds me to assume and respect the complexity of others.

TRANS*PERSPECTIVE: DEAN KOTULA ON THE WORD *TRANSGENDER*

I don't like the word *transgender*. Gender refers to behavior and whether or not someone is masculine or feminine. I have never crossed genders. I always had a masculine presentation. Even if I had had feminine gestures or attributes, I would have recognized myself as being male (albeit feminine). The point here is that no one needed to tell me I was male, nor did they need to tell me what to wear, [what to] think, or how to act to convince the world. Nothing changed when I transitioned except that my body was masculinized further through the use of hormones and surgery. I am a transsexual, having gone from a female body to a male body.

CHAPTER SIX

DAVE GAER

Having performed [in drag] *as a woman for many years, I find that I have incorporated aspects of "woman" into my everyday interactions. In the past, I would pay careful attention to perform "male" in interactions, and especially at work. The more I performed, the more I realized that I was ignoring a part of myself, the parts typically defined as female, and that it was a lot of work to not be myself. I would say that I am no longer playing with the concept of gender, but I am truly able to just be ME.*

—Dave

Dave Gaer is a forty-something professional educator and gay man who grew up in the western United States. He has recently moved to the South after living in the Midwest and West for many years. He performs in drag as a character he calls MiMi, and he has helped others learn to become drag performers. In describing himself, he says, "I like to direct theatre productions, coach speech and debate, and in what little spare time I do have, I love to camp and fish, spending as much time in the outdoors as I can. Fishing is the most relaxing activity there is, and it's what I do to unwind, and I usually can be found reading a book at the same time." He also spends a great deal of time with family and friends.

DAVE AND MIMI

Dave's drag persona, MiMi, emerged when Dave was in graduate school in the Midwest.

I began my stint as MiMi in the early 1990s. Originally, it was meant to be a Halloween-only gig. A friend dressed me up as Divine [the stage name of Harris Glenn Milstead, an American actor, singer, and drag queen], one of the first and most famous gender benders. I had a blast that Halloween and actually placed in a costume contest at a local bar. What developed from there was an encouragement from friends to pursue drag and to perform in a show doing lip-synch-style drag. It took me a while, and with my theatre background, it seemed like another style of performance that fit with what I liked to do. I performed in one show and was hooked.

My next experience was in a pageant in the same town, and while it was nerve-wracking, I had a blast. At that point, I was [ready to do drag] and loved the idea of performing as MiMi. As MiMi developed, I became more of an impersonator [using the character of MiMi Bobeck from *The Drew Carey Show* (1995–2004) as inspiration]. [My MiMi] was brash and sassy, and audiences loved her.

Family members were very supportive of Dave, which surprised him, because he assumed they wouldn't be. "I underestimated my family and didn't tell them right away [about MiMi]. . . . I assumed that they would not understand, and that they would judge me as a person for wanting to dress and to perform as a woman. I was wrong, and they even laughed about how much [my MiMi] looked like a certain family member."

Public reactions to Dave's persona can be more complicated. He says:

People often comment that they are amazed at the transformation that I make from "male" to "female." I try to present as naturally as possible and often can fool people. I am a bald, bearded man, and the "woman" they see when I dress/perform is a convincing and shocking transformation.

Once on the way to [a] party, the hostess called and asked

(a friend and me, both of us in drag) to stop and get ice. We stopped at the local convenience store, and while in the store, a gentleman behind us whistled at us and said, "Damn, you are hot." When I turned around, with my unshaven face and deep bass voice, and said, "Thank you!" he was shocked. It brought laughter from everyone in the store. He ended up talking to us after the fact and related how embarrassed he was. He was confused by our appearance and by the physical presentation of "woman." He remarked that we walked in heels like women. My friend and I still laugh about this to this day!

PERFORMING GENDER

Performing as a woman has led Dave to new ideas about his genders. He says:

I hate pantyhose and heels! But I have a much deeper appreciation for what being "woman" means and what females go through to transform into the expectation of what being female means. Drag, I believe, has performed an essential function in my exploration of self. Every person has to play with concepts of what it means to be male or female and what society expects from us as such. When we rely on social norms to determine who we are, we often get caught, even chastised, for behaviors that place us outside of the norms.

By performing as "woman" on stage, I believe I began to understand the concept that there is no "woman" or "man," but simply people with aspects of both, and that no one should shy away from either. I can be effeminate at times, through gesture or mannerism, I can cry in public if I feel it, and I can just wade through this world being myself and not worrying about what others think. Performing as MiMi has been a big part of letting this happen. After thirty years, I am finally comfortable with just being ME.

CHAPTER SEVEN

TRANS*HISTORY NARRATIVES

Trans* individuals have always been a part of human history. Both men and women have taken on characteristics of the opposite gender. Sometimes the change is for practical reasons. For example, in many cultures, women couldn't fight in wars, but men could, so Joan of Arc (1412–1431) dressed as a man to fight for France. Sometimes it was for theatrical performances. For example, in Shakespeare's time, men played women's parts on the English stage. Sometimes it was simply a matter of personal preference.

GODS, PRIESTS, AND ADMIRALS

Gender-flexible individuals lived in early human cultures. Archaeologists in the Czech Republic have discovered the five-thousand-year-old remains of a person who was likely gender flexible. The ancient Greeks also had a tradition of gender

Joan of Arc donned military garb to fight for France in the Hundred Years' War (1337–1453). This miniature portrait in oil of the French heroine in battle gear was painted in about 1485.

flexibility. For example, during ancient Greek feasts and rites to celebrate Dionysus, the god of wine, women wore strap-on phalluses (penises), and men wore women's clothing. Similarly, the Greek goddess Athena—the goddess of intellect, arts, and warfare—was often depicted as a male warrior.

Another early group of trans* people were eunuchs, who were common in ancient Egypt, ancient Rome, the early Persian Empire, and many different Asian cultures. Eunuchs were castrated males (some cultures removed the penis as well as the testicles) who had many functions in ancient societies, often as servants or slaves and sometimes as guards for women. Eunuch priests known as Galli played a role in religious practices in ancient Rome as early as 204 BCE. They wore women's clothing, jewelry, long bleached hair, and heavy makeup. Much later, in the fifteenth century CE, the Chinese eunuch admiral warrior Zheng He (1371–1433, birth name Ma He) navigated the Chinese treasure fleet around much of the world.

ROYAL GENDER BENDING

The Roman emperor Elagabalus (203–222 CE) may have been one of the first trans* individuals in a public position. Some sources say he married both men and women, wore makeup, dressed as a woman, and offered surgeons a great deal of money to equip him with female genitalia.

Another notable example of a trans* head of state is Queen Christina of Sweden, who ruled during the seventeenth century. Some sources speculate that Christina was an intersex individual. Reports agree that Christina had both feminine and masculine physical traits. In a time when women were supposed to be demure and quiet, Christina was boisterous and engaged in worldly affairs. After Christina gave up the throne (partially because Christina had decided not to marry and produce an heir), Christina sometimes went by the name Count Dohna. Unlike most European women of the age, Christina spent much time in the company of men (including popes and cardinals), enjoying pursuits in the male-dominated realms of arts and sciences. At this time in history, women were not allowed these privileges.

GENDER IN WARTIME

War is often a trigger for a gender shift for women. As a young teen, French heroine Joan of Arc responded to a religious vision directing her to drive out English occupiers of France during the Hundred Years' War (1337–1453). Joining the French army, she cut her hair short and wore men's clothing. Interpretations differ as to whether she wore men's clothes because she wanted to or because it was prudent for her safety. In an all-male army, she would likely have feared physical assaults such as rape. When she was discovered to be cross-dressing, her superiors demanded that she give up her male clothing, and she agreed to do so. However, the army leaders did not provide her with gear appropriate to females, so she donned her male clothing again. Joan of Arc was ultimately accused of heresy (acting against established religious doctrine) and of cross-dressing and was burned at the stake in 1431.

Centuries later, on the other side of the Atlantic Ocean, Deborah Sampson served in the Continental Army during the American Revolutionary War (1775–1783) under the name Robert Shurtleff. Careful physical examinations were not required by the military in early wars, so the army simply accepted her claim to be male. Sampson took ill during the conflict and required medical attention. The doctor tending to her discovered her biological sex but did not reveal her secret.

After the war, Sampson married and had children. She also petitioned the State of Massachusetts to be paid for her service in the military. The General Court of Massachusetts agreed to her request, saying she had served honorably and bravely while maintaining her virtue as a woman. As she got older, she petitioned to receive a military pension to better support her family and her farm. It took almost twenty years and several petitions to the US Congress, but she was finally granted a pension similar to that of other male soldiers.

Many women also served as soldiers, spies, or male nurses in the American Civil War (1861–1865). The few whose names are known include Frances Clalin (Jack Williams), Sarah Pritchard (Samuel "Sammy" Blalock), and Sarah Edmonds (Franklin "Flint" Thompson). All three of these women served in the Union army, donning male uniforms and, in some cases, taking on expected male behaviors such as gambling, drinking, smoking, and swearing. They were all considered model soldiers. Each resumed her life as a traditional female homemaker after the war was over.

Jennie Hodgers also enlisted in the Union army during the Civil War. She chose to continue living as her male self, Albert Cashier, after the war. As a man, Cashier was legally allowed to vote and to claim a veteran's pension. His secret was discovered after the war when he broke his leg, but the physician who treated him kept his secret. As Albert got older, he developed dementia and was moved to a state hospital for the insane. When nursing attendants discovered Albert had a female body, he was forced to wear a dress. Nevertheless, when Albert died in 1915, "Albert D. J. Cashier" was engraved on his tombstone. In the 1970s, a second tombstone with both of Albert's names was placed next to the first one.

Jennie Hodgers served as Albert Cashier in the Union army's 95th Illinois Regiment during the American Civil War. Hodgers kept the male identity after the war ended.

Men have also been known to dress as women during war, though usually to escape service or capture. In the mythical story of the Greek hero Achilles, famous as a warrior in the Trojan War, Achilles' mother disguises him as a young girl to avoid sending him off to battle. He is eventually discovered, reclaims a male identity, and leads the Greeks to victory. This episode of the Achilles myth was later popularized in paintings, plays, ballet, and especially opera. Another famous case is that of Charles Edward Stuart, known as Bonnie Prince Charlie. Charles led a rebellion against the British government in the mid-1700s in an unsuccessful attempt to restore his family to the throne. Facing capture in Scotland, he dressed as a female servant to flee pursuing government forces.

GENDER IN INDIGENOUS CULTURES

Some indigenous cultures preserve the trans*-friendly gender roles their cultures have held for thousands of years. In fact, the languages of many indigenous cultures have words for individuals known as two-spirits, or people who express a gender identity that combines both male and female gender roles. (Previously, two-spirits were referred to as *berdaches*, but that term is now considered insulting.) As examples, the Lakota word for a two-spirit person is *winkte*, the Navajo word is *nádleehí*, the Crow word is *boté*, the Potawatomi word is *m'netokwe*, and the Zuni word is *lhamana*.

In many tribes' histories, two-spirit individuals had mixed gender roles and often wore the clothes of the gender opposite their sex. Sometimes two-spirits expressed both gender roles simultaneously. A two-spirit individual who was biologically male but female-gendered might have fought in war and had access to male sweat lodges but still performed domestic tasks such as cooking. In some tribes, these individuals could have romantic and family partnerships with either sex. They were often viewed as possessing extraordinary gifts. For example, some tribes viewed two-spirits as gifted healers. In other tribes, two-spirit individuals were honored with the responsibility of making sacred items such as pottery or dance regalia. Individuals who are two-spirit in the modern world may have mixed or single gender roles, depending on the tribe.

Barcheeampe (Biawacheeitche, Woman Chief, or Pine Leaf) was born into the Gros Ventre tribe around 1800 and was captured by the Apsáalooke (Crow) when she was ten. As a two-spirit individual, she participated with superior skill in masculine pursuits such as hunting and fighting. Even though she dressed as a woman, she led many successful war parties. Before she was killed by the Gros Ventre in 1854, she was considered a high-ranking leader among the Crow.

We'wha, born into a male body, was a two-spirit member of the Zuni people. She was an accomplished weaver and potter. As an official representative of her tribe, she made a trip to Washington, DC, in 1886 as part of a larger cultural mission, organized by American anthropologists, to introduce indigenous peoples to the nation's capital. While there, she socialized with politicians and high-ranking government officials, the social elite, and President Grover Cleveland. She also demonstrated her weaving skills and worked with anthropologists at the Smithsonian Institution.

Zuni artisan We'wha visited Washington, DC, in 1886. The two-spirit representative became a celebrity and was the subject of portraits such as this one by American government photographer John K. Hillers during that visit.

GENDER FLUIDITY AROUND THE WORLD

In Thailand, *kathoey* are a group of trans* individuals who include gay men, men who dress as women, trans* women, a third gender combining male and female, and intersex individuals. Some kathoey undergo feminizing procedures, such as breast implants, and some wear makeup while others do not. Generally, kathoey are accepted in Thai culture and work as models, hairstylists, or cabaret performers. The most internationally recognized kathoey is Parinya Charoenphol (Kiatbusaba), or Nong Tum (Thoom), a Thai kickboxer. Her life was the basis for the 2003 Thai film *Beautiful Boxer*.

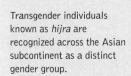

Transgender individuals known as *hijra* are recognized across the Asian subcontinent as a distinct gender group.

In India and other nations of South Asia, hijra are a group of trans* individuals with a long historical tradition in the region. Similar to kathoey, they are biological males who adopt feminine gender roles and dress. Sometimes hijra are castrated and become eunuchs, and a few are intersex. Hijra renounce their sexuality and do not participate in sexual activity for themselves, though some do sex work to generate income. In Bangladesh they are now considered their own gender, distinct from men and women.

Some hijra live in all-hijra communities, which tend to protect the safety of these individuals, who often encounter job, housing, and health-care discrimination. However, hijra have a special place in the Hindu and Muslim faiths. Often viewed as possessing magical powers, they are sometimes called upon to bless weddings and the births of baby boys to bring good luck and fertility.

In Albania and other Balkan countries, women called *burneshas* (sworn virgins) take permanent vows of celibacy in order to carry out male roles in their culture. By making the choice to switch gender roles, the sworn virgins are allowed to inherit property, care for widows, and act as the head of a household. As a sworn virgin, the woman is also allowed to smoke, carry a gun, use a male name, and wear male clothes. She also avoids being sold into marriage. The Albanian sworn virgin is believed to be the only formalized, socially defined cross-dressing role in European cultures.

The dancer Jin Xing *(below)* is a pioneer in China because she is one of the few trans* women recognized by the Chinese government. Jin dances in ballet and modern dance productions, and she is also a choreographer and actress. She runs Shanghai's Jin Xing Dance Theatre, one of China's few nongovernmental dance troupes. Jin had gender confirmation surgery in 1995. Her decision shocked China: the country's best male dancer had become female. Jin adopted children in 2000 and married a German man not long after she became a mother.

In a culture that values conformity above many other human traits, Jin knows that being herself was a huge risk to take. Her bold decision has helped China grant civil rights to other transgender people, allowing them to change government identity cards and passports to their preferred gender. Jin knows that her culture may eventually come to a better acceptance of trans* individuals, but it will take time: "The day I came out as a woman to society, I said, 'Okay, I give myself fifty years' time, I will tell the society who I am.'" Until those fifty years pass, she is content to be herself and wait for broader social acceptance to come.

CHAPTER EIGHT

BROOKE WILCOXSON

What do I love about being intersex? It's very unique, and it's something I want to talk about, so then people say, "Oh, that's what it means. Oh, that's how an intersex person is." I think it's an honor. It's nice to be the person who can help others understand. I am a good role model, and [our] culture needs to know who we are.

—Brooke

Brooke Wilcoxson is in her early twenties. She grew up in the South and is now living in a major East Coast metropolitan area, where she attended college. She's applying for graduate school in social work because she wants to become a licensed marriage and family therapist. Brooke is passionate about her schoolwork and helping others. She loves to draw and paint and is also devoted to music. Brooke is deaf, so she hears music differently than others do. She loves to sing, write songs, and play the piano. In fact, she often sings at weddings and funerals.

BODY CHANGES

When Brooke entered puberty, her clitoris grew into a micropenis. Afterward, Brooke discovered that her sex chromosomes are XXY rather than the more common female combination of two X chromosomes. With the addition of the Y (male) chromosome, her body makes more testosterone than estrogen, and the testosterone production began at puberty. Although Brooke has a micropenis and facial hair that grows quickly (she shaves regularly), her biological and gender identity remain female. She also has fully developed breasts. All the same, Brooke dislikes wearing feminine clothes and feels more comfortable in masculine clothing styles.

It took Brooke and her family a while to make sense of her biology: "When I first found out, I went through hell. It took me a while to accept myself and to learn to live my life." Brooke says:

> When my mom first found out, she said "Oh my God, my daughter's half man and half woman," and I said, "No, Mom, I'm a woman, but I'm different below the waist." I thought about having surgery for the sake of my mother. My mom wanted me to take a pill to bring up my estrogen level, but it was too late [because the changes had already happened].
>
> I talked to God, and I especially asked, "Why did you make me this way?" I also talked to my grandfather, who was a pastor, and he told me God created man and woman separately, not in between. I was angry at God for a long time. But then I told my grandfather, "Because you preach God's word, and God doesn't judge, you can't judge me," and that backed him down.

Brooke felt a lot of shame at first and distanced herself from many people. But when she met her transgender aunt, she started to feel more confident.

> I realized it was not my fault that I am intersex. My aunt told me I couldn't have surgery [to change the micropenis] just because my mother wanted me to be a "normal woman." I had to do it for me, and I didn't want to do it. I know I'm a female on the outside, but sometimes I feel like a male on the inside, but I don't feel like I want to change my actual sex. When I talked to my aunt, I asked her, "Do you think I should change?" My aunt said I was able to have both worlds because of the way I currently am, and I would know if I needed to change.

Brooke's aunt helped her understand that her essential self will never change: "I will always be Brooke, and I love who I am. If I am intersex, so be it."

SHARING STORIES

Sharing her story with others is one of Brooke's great joys, although she was initially hesitant to do so. She realizes she is one of a kind. She says, "I [am] the only African American female intersex person [people] might meet, so they need me to represent and educate them as to what intersex is and what it's like living as that person."

Brooke feels deeply honored to be able to share who she is in an educational setting. And she has much to talk about, because she has many intersecting identities—she is an African American woman, a lesbian, a deaf individual, and an intersex individual. People are always curious to hear more about her life.

> When I talk on panels and tell my story, I get so much support—
> "You're awesome, You're brave!" Lots of people don't know what
> *intersex* and *hermaphrodite* mean, so it's been very wonderful and
> enriching because I'm willing to tell my story. I am African
> American, I am female, and I am deaf, but people say, "No Brooke,
> we see that. What's the real story? Share more, share more." I also
> don't want others explaining my story—I want to tell it myself.

In a social or a dating situation, Brooke says she's a little bit slower to talk about being intersex. She explains, "I have to see who you are, and see if you support the LGBT community, before I will tell you I'm intersex. I have to get to know you more deeply."

GOALS AND DREAMS

When Brooke thinks about her future, she's very excited, because she knows she can contribute to the world in many ways. She wants to pursue a PhD and write a book about creating good marriages. Brooke knows that teens and young adults will need her positivity. "I want to become a young adult mentor, because I've noticed that these young kids really need help—young girls getting pregnant, young men going to jail. I want to be there for them." Brooke is determined to be a positive influence, no matter how her future unfolds.

Part of Brooke's optimism about her life and her future comes from her enormous spiritual faith. She says:

> God made me this way for a reason. God needs me to represent the African American community, the LGBT community, and the deaf community. My anger grew my faith. I finally said to God, "You made me this way, so I'm going to praise you for that." I go to church every Sunday and thank God for making me like this because I would have never had the wonderful experiences I've had without being intersex. . . . Whenever someone asks, "Why are you this way?" I say, "I don't know, ask God."

CHAPTER NINE

TRANS*HEALTH COMPLEXITIES

Trans* individuals do not always have equal access to health care, and when they do, many do not receive quality, respectful treatment from medical professionals. In some cases, this lack of quality care comes from a lack of knowledge of trans* health issues on the part of medical providers. In other cases, trans* patients lack confidence in the medical system and its ability to recognize and meet trans* needs because of previous negative interactions.

STUDYING TRANS* HEALTH CARE

According to a landmark study conducted in 2008 and officially released in 2010 by the National Center for Transgender Equality, trans* and gender-nonconforming individuals face enormous barriers in accessing medical care. The survey was conducted nationwide, on paper and online, and included 6,540 individuals from all fifty states, the District of Columbia, Puerto Rico, Guam, and the US Virgin Islands.

Many significant findings emerged from the study, including these:

- The biggest hurdles to accessing health care are refusal of care because of trans* identity (19 percent of respondents), harassment and violence in the medical setting (28 percent), and lack of provider knowledge (50 percent).
- Many participants postpone medical care when they are sick or injured due to discrimination when receiving care (28 percent) or the inability to afford care (48 percent).

- Verbal harassment in a doctor's office, emergency room, or other medical setting was reported by 24 percent of respondents, and 2 percent of the respondents reported being physically attacked in a doctor's office.
- Trans* individuals have more than four times the national average of human immunodeficiency syndrome (HIV) infection (2.6 percent in the sample, compared with 0.6 percent in the general population).
- More than one-quarter of the respondents misused drugs or alcohol specifically to cope with the emotional toll of discrimination. Cigarette smokers make up 30 percent of the respondents, compared to 20.6 percent of the general US population. Smoking may also be used as a coping tool for dealing with discrimination.
- Of the respondents, 41 percent reported attempting suicide, compared to 1.6 percent of the general population. Risk factors for suicide include unemployment, low income, and sexual or physical assault—all related to trans* identity.

Complicating these statistics is the fact that study participants were less likely to have access to insurance, which typically leads to poor overall health care. Additionally, individuals of color were less likely to receive quality health care, as were those who do not visually conform to gender expectations. Individuals who were open about their gender transition in a health-care setting ran a higher risk of harassment or discrimination.

As a result of its findings, the study recommends doctor education and insurance coverage as major priorities within health-care reform. It also supports disciplinary action (according to the standards of their profession) for doctors who discriminate against trans* individuals. The study also notes that an end to violence against trans* individuals should be a major public health initiative.

SUICIDE

Trans* individuals in the United States are at particularly high risk of suicide. Trans* individuals who have been bullied are at higher risk, especially when the bullies are teachers. Of trans* people who attempt suicide, 44 percent are visual nonconformers. Also, 44 percent are people who are out about their trans* status. Those who have medically and surgically transitioned have higher rates of attempted suicide than those who have not.

Education, income, and employment status also correlate with suicide rates. Trans* individuals with less money and less education are at a higher risk, and 51 percent of trans* individuals who attempt suicide are unemployed. Assault also correlates with suicide. In the National Center for Transgender Equality study, 61 percent of physical assault survivors had attempted suicide, as had 65 percent of sexual assault survivors.

Writer and teacher Cary Gabriel Costello, a trans* man, shared a story about trans* suicide on his blog. When a suicidal friend called the National Suicide Prevention Helpline, the man who answered the phone talked to the friend for several minutes. Costello says:

> When [the helpline representative] was talking with her about whether there were friends she could turn to, she told him she was a trans* woman, and that that had limited her social circle. There was a pause, and then the man at the National Suicide Prevention Helpline hung up on her. It is transphobia like this that explains that 41 percent attempted suicide rate.

Costello's friend survived—in part, he says, because she laughed at the awful irony of a suicide hotline worker hanging up on her.

THE TRANSITION PROCESS

Once a trans* individual makes the personal decision to use hormones or gender confirmation surgery to guide their gender presentation, that person will usually be involved with both mental health practitioners and medical doctors. Often the trans* individual must be given a diagnosis of gender dysphoria from a mental health practitioner before treatment can begin. After the diagnosis, the trans* person usually seeks treatment with hormones and/or androgen blockers, all of which can be prescribed by an endocrinologist or a related specialist. Medical professionals usually prescribe hormones if the person in transition is already living openly as the gender to which that person wants to medically transition. Eventually, if the trans* person desires and can afford surgery, doctors make referrals to specialists so gender confirmation surgeries can be performed.

If a trans* individual decides to make a medical transition, the process might begin in a hometown doctor's office or a major medical center in a big city. The World Professional Association for Transgender Health created a standards of care document for doctors who treat all gender-nonconforming individuals. Any doctor, in a small town or a large city, can use this document to aid in giving transitioning individuals the best care possible.

Transition progress varies from individual to individual. Hormones change an individual's body shape, hair growth, voice, fat distribution, muscle mass, and other physical characteristics at different rates. Surgeries will be scheduled at various times depending on finances, desires, and an individual's preparation. Medical (hormonal) or surgical transition does involve health risks. Cross-sex hormones can cause serious and sometimes fatal complications, including a heightened risk of cancer. Of course, any surgery has risks, and gender confirmation surgeries are no exception.

Trans* individuals also suffer health risks from not having access to medical or surgical transition care. Sometimes hormones are denied to trans* individuals because of a lack of money, the lack of access to the signature of an important doctor, or any number of other reasons.

Sometimes individuals don't have access to larger cities with medical facilities to treat gender dysphoria because of geography or lack of money for travel. This lack and/or denial of care can create other risks, including a higher chance of depression, anxiety, and suicidal thoughts or behavior.

MORALS AND MEDICINE: THE CASE OF ROBERT EADS

Robert Eads was a trans* man who lived in Georgia. Eads transitioned in the late 1980s, when he was in his forties. He received testosterone and a double mastectomy. At that time, his doctors counseled that he did not need a hysterectomy and oophorectomy because he was close to menopause, when the female body naturally stops producing estrogen.

In 1996 Eads experienced heavy vaginal bleeding and sought emergency medical treatment. He was diagnosed with ovarian cancer, which may have been linked to his testosterone treatment. However, gynecologists refused to treat Eads. They claimed that treating him would be bad for their reputation and harmful for the other female patients in their practice. In 1997 Eads found doctors at the Medical College of Georgia to treat him, and he underwent aggressive surgery, chemotherapy, and radiation. However, by this stage, the cancer had progressed too far and could not be controlled. Eads died in 1999 from ovarian cancer at the age of fifty-three.

CHAPTER TEN

JULIA KELEHER

The thing that I love most about the transgender part of myself is the ability to be myself. I love everything about my gender. I feel the most comfortable in masculine clothing, and I love to wear dress clothes like ties and bowties.

—Julia

Julia is an academic professional who works in student affairs at a medium-sized college in a western state. She was raised in the Midwest during the 1980s and the 1990s and has "an awesome job" that allows her to work with LGBTQA students. She says, "I am also proud to call myself a nerd. I love comic books, TV, and movies. My two favorite TV shows are *The Simpsons* and *Buffy the Vampire Slayer*. I have yet to find a person who can beat me at *Simpsons* trivia."

GROWING UP

Since she was a young child, Julia has been aware of her gender identity. "At five, I wanted a Mohawk, and the little boy I told said that girls couldn't have a Mohawk." She didn't understand why she had to play softball just because she was a girl. She wanted to play baseball, like the boys, even though her mother thought baseball was too rough for her. Julia says:

> It has always been hard for me to fit into social expectations of what a biological female is supposed to be. I lived outside as a kid and rode my bike everywhere. I loved my Huffy [bike], which was

for boys. I wanted to have short hair and wanted to wear boys' clothing. Most of my friends were boys, and I didn't mind getting dirty. I have never been tough, however. I didn't like to fight, and confrontation has always frightened me. I could get away with my physical weakness because I am biologically female.

BEING GENDERQUEER

Julia isn't comfortable defining herself as a man or as a woman. She clarifies her thinking:

I don't think I am really a man or a woman. I'm in between the two terms. I've always called myself a woman or female because that's what my physical sex is, but it's never really felt connected to either term. I just like to be called Julia and not have a gender marker, but that's hard to do in our society.

When she went to college, Julia remembers that "buzzing my hair off was one of the most liberating experiences of my life. It felt like I was finally living outside of the societal expectations that I was forced to live with since I was a small child." Her mother supports Julia's genderqueer identity. In fact, for Christmas one year, Julia's mother bought her boxer briefs, just as she had done for Julia's brother.

Julia has considered taking hormones and having surgery to make her body more masculine, but she prefers to wait and see. As she says, "My gender identity often changes and morphs." Julia strives to be a role model for her LGBTQA college students, and her genderqueer identity is a huge help in that task, because she is an example of someone who's comfortable living outside the gender binary. Because Julia is free to express her gender, her students are encouraged to do the same simply through her example. As Julia notes, "I don't know who I would be if I couldn't fully express my gender the way I want to. I have the freedom to be as masculine as I want, and that's something that I truly enjoy."

Just like cisgender individuals, trans* individuals express sexual orientation, sexual identity, and sexual preferences across a wide spectrum. People who are trans* may consider themselves straight, gay, bisexual, asexual, or pansexual (being attracted to multiple genders and sexual orientations). And just as with cisgender individuals, sexual identity and orientation can shift over time for trans* individuals.

Julia comments that she sometimes faces uncomfortable moments in public when people can't figure out her gender identity. But she has a great response. She says:

At times, it can make me feel like I am some sort of freak or weirdo when people stare at me. This was really hard for me for a long time. There was a certain point where I just decided to ignore the looks. It's not my problem that my gender identity makes people feel uncomfortable. I'm just being myself. If I get a lot of stares or snickers, I just smile back. Nothing unnerves people more than kindness when they are making fun of you or judging you.

CHAPTER ELEVEN

TRANS*LIFE CHALLENGES

Living within a trans* identity can be a complicated situation for many different reasons. Cisgender individuals are often unaware of the impact gender has on their lives, but trans* individuals have to think about their gender every day.

GENDER POLICING

Human beings often judge others by how they look. Individuals (trans* or not) who don't fit into the gender binary are often monitored (policed) by others for not being "normal." Because the gender binary in the United States is rigid and gender norms can be hard to fit into, individuals who don't fit those norms are often called out, shamed, or ridiculed for not fitting in. Often this policing starts in childhood, when others may try to guide a gender-nonconforming child into dressing as their assigned sex or prevent them from playing with particular kinds of toys. Gender policing can happen through comments (such as "Oh, look, a man in a dress"), through verbal harassment of the trans* person (such as "You're just pretending to be a guy!"), or by intentionally using the wrong pronouns to refer to an individual. All gender policing marginalizes trans* individuals, relegating them to powerlessness or low social status.

Trans* individuals are often judged, sensationalized, and policed in the media as well. For example, reports on trans* crime victims have used the wrong pronouns to identify the victims or have focused on details that prioritize the individual's gender over the crime committed against them. Movies and television also tend to portray trans* individuals in one-dimensional ways. If a trans* character is included in a show, they might have a small part as a sex worker or a criminal (negative roles in American culture) instead of as someone's spouse or brother. Rarely are they portrayed as individuals with multifaceted lives.

TRANS*INJUSTICE: DISCRIMINATION AND BULLYING

Trans* individuals are at high risk for discrimination and violence. Sometimes it's someone calling out a rude name from a passing car or assaulting you for your trans* identity. Sometimes it's a doctor refusing to treat you for routine medical care or it's a landlord refusing to rent to you. Sometimes it's losing your job or not getting hired in the first place. This unfair and violent treatment is based in transphobia.

Sometimes discrimination strikes in the middle of an emergency. In Washington, DC, in 1995, trans* woman Tyra Hunter was injured in a hit-and-run car accident. When the paramedics began working on her, they discovered she had a penis and began ridiculing her instead of treating her. Hunter later died at the hospital as a result of her injuries. Even though eyewitnesses confirmed the ridicule from the emergency personnel, no charges were brought against the paramedics.

Trans* individuals typically face discrimination and bullying from a young age. According to a report from the National Center for Transgender Equality, 78 percent of trans* students in grades K through 12 reported harassment by students, teachers, or staff. Some students encountered physical violence (35 percent) or sexual assault (12 percent). Some students were even expelled from school because of their trans* identity (6 percent).

A trans* individual's gender identity may also lessen their access to important resources, such as jobs, health care, safe living spaces, and education. If a trans* person is also a person of color, or is gay, lesbian, or bisexual, or has a disability, they may have even less access to these resources. The same goes for a trans* person who is not a citizen of the United States.

Antidiscrimination laws are in place in some states to protect trans* individuals from unfair treatment. But in other states, it remains legal to reject trans* individuals for jobs, housing, and health-care services because of their gender identity. According to the American Civil Liberties Union,

> California, Colorado, Hawaii, Illinois, Iowa, Maine, Minnesota, New Jersey, New Mexico, Oregon, Rhode Island, Vermont, Washington and the District of Columbia all have laws [protecting trans* individuals]. Their protections vary. Minnesota's law bans discrimination in employment, housing, education and public accommodations; Hawaii's covers only housing. At least 93 cities and counties have passed their own laws prohibiting gender identity discrimination including Phoenix, Atlanta, Louisville, New Orleans, Cincinnati, Pittsburgh, Indianapolis, Dallas, and Buffalo.

In the summer of 2013, California governor Jerry Brown signed the School Success and Opportunity Act (AB1266) into law, ensuring that trans* youth have equal access to bathrooms, locker rooms, sports teams, physical education classes, and other school events and facilities based on their self-identified gender. This new law is a significant victory for trans* justice. In the fall of 2013, a national Employment Non-Discrimination Act passed a vote in the US Senate. The bill prevents workplace discrimination on the basis of sexual orientation or gender identity. If the bill passes in the US House of Representatives, it will mark a very significant step forward for trans* rights in America.

VIOLENCE AND TRANS* INDIVIDUALS

Trans* individuals of all identities are vulnerable to a high incidence of violence in their lives. Around the world, an estimated 265 trans* individuals were murdered in 2012, and 238 murders were recorded in 2013. Any unreported murders would add to those numbers.

In response to violence against trans* individuals, Gwendolyn Ann Smith founded the International Transgender Day of Remembrance in 1999. Observed on November 20 every year, the day honors all individuals who have lost their lives to trans*-motivated violence. Smith started the remembrance in honor of African American trans* woman Rita Hester, who was murdered in Massachusetts in November 1998. Smith said:

> The Transgender Day of Remembrance seeks to highlight the losses we face due to anti-transgender bigotry and violence. I am no stranger to the need to fight for our rights, and the right to simply exist is first and foremost. With so many seeking to erase transgender people—sometimes in the most brutal ways possible—it is vitally important that those we lose are remembered, and that we continue to fight for justice.

Sometimes trans* individuals fight back. CeCe McDonald, a young African American trans* woman, was verbally and then physically assaulted in June 2011 while living in Minneapolis, Minnesota. Three individuals outside a bar taunted CeCe for her trans* identity as well as her racial identity as she and her friends walked past on their way to a nearby grocery store. Though CeCe and her friends tried to walk away, a violent fight ensued. One of the attackers, Dean Schmitz, was killed during the fight.

During the fight, CeCe received a stab wound that punctured her cheek and her salivary gland and required many stitches. For CeCe's injuries, Dean Schmitz's ex-girlfriend Molly Flaherty pled guilty to third-degree assault and was sentenced to six months' jail time and probation.

CeCe was charged with the second-degree murder of Dean Schmitz. To shorten her time in prison, she accepted a plea agreement of second-degree manslaughter. (Had a jury found against CeCe, she might have spent decades in jail.) CeCe was sentenced in June 2012 and was assigned to serve her time in a men's prison. (Though prison officials are empowered to make exceptions, trans* individuals are usually incarcerated based on their assigned sex at birth.) CeCe was released in January 2014.

CeCe is an upbeat person, and she communicated with her supporters through blog posts while she was in prison. During her birthday month in 2013, she posted this observation:

> I'll be turning 25 this month, and for me being in prison for saving my own life is worth celebrating another year, even if it's in a f****d up environment. I feel blessed—no, I am blessed to say that I've lived for a quarter of a century. That through my trials and tribulations, through my life's quarrels, that when I never thought I'd make it past the age of sixteen, I triumphed over all obstacles and that in itself is a victory. So for me, this is a major milestone, especially considering the violence against trans* women and the injustices of a faulty "judicial system" . . . I can say that through all the adversity I faced over the course of time I lived so far, I've evolved and accomplished more than I would have ever imagined. And I can only go up from here!

PRIVATE CHELSEA MANNING'S GENDER BATTLE

Private Chelsea Manning was known as Private Bradley Manning until the day after she was sentenced to serve thirty-five years in a federal military prison. On August 21, 2013, Manning was convicted for her role in the WikiLeaks scandal. She had begun providing classified US Army documents to the WikiLeaks website in 2010. Manning's role in the scandal led to a charge of espionage against her for sending more than seven hundred thousand confidential military and US State Department documents to the WikiLeaks website while she worked as an intelligence analyst in Iraq.

Manning had been diagnosed with gender dysphoria before her trial, but at the time of her sentencing, the US Army reevaluated her and declared she would not receive hormone replacement therapy or gender reassignment surgery in prison. She will most likely be allowed to change her name, but she will not be allowed to dress as a woman in prison. Manning is serving her time at the United States Disciplinary Barracks (known as Leavenworth), a federal prison for male inmates at Fort Leavenworth, Kansas. She plans to go to court to fight for her desire to receive hormone treatment.

CHAPTER TWELVE

NATASHA AND NANCY

The biggest thing I love about being trans* is the unique perspective I get. Most people only see life through the lenses of male or female, whereas I see things a little bit through both. I get a different perspective that I feel is a huge strength when it comes to thinking about things critically and approaching problems.

—Natasha

Natasha and Nancy have been together since 2010, and marriage is in their future. Natasha describes herself as smart and "empirically centered," meaning she likes facts and numbers. She lives in a small midwestern city and is majoring in psychology as she works toward a law degree. Someday she hopes to represent other transgender individuals in their legal disputes. Natasha is at the very beginning of her transition, and she knows that "fully transition[ing] and liv[ing] full-time as a woman [will help] build a stronger rapport with potential clients who need legal assistance as they transition." She and Nancy identify as "somewhat nerdy," and they like to read, listen to music, game, and watch movies. They also work at their local Renaissance festival.

CLOTHES AND IDENTITY

As a child, when Natasha was Nathan, she'd see a girl's outfit and think, "I would look good in that." She started dressing as a girl in private when she was nine or ten, but didn't really understand "what was going on until fourteenish." At that point, Natasha explored her transsexual side through research for about ten years before she was able to begin her transition. Sometimes, while Natasha was Nathan, she would wear dresses at the Renaissance festival. Now, Natasha dresses full-time as a woman, though she has yet to begin hormone therapy.

Both Natasha and Nancy identify as genderqueer, although Natasha also identifies with the word *transsexual*. Nancy says she was questioning her own sexuality (though not her gender) before she fell in love with Natasha, but that "being in a relationship with [Natasha] has helped me reach decisions that I might have taken much longer to reach had she not been in my life. Truthfully, I am still questioning [my sexuality] a little bit, [and] I don't know if I will ever stop either."

FRIENDS, FAMILY, AND SUPPORT

Natasha says that "for the most part, I feel comfortable in being out, but I don't actively bring up my transness either. I still get nervous around people, but for the most part I have stopped caring about their reactions. I have come to the realization that I have to live for myself, not for the perceptions of others."

Natasha and Nancy have some support from their families, although Natasha's parents still don't totally understand Natasha's gender. Natasha and Nancy told Nancy's family about their relationship while Natasha was presenting to the world as Nathan. They explained that Natasha was a transsexual woman, and some members of Nancy's family tried to break the couple up. However, some family members on both sides were very supportive. As time goes on, family members are becoming more comfortable with the relationship.

Natasha and Nancy's friends are supportive of the pair. According to Natasha, "I've had some great interactions with friends. You never know how someone is going to react to the news of you being trans until you tell them."

Do you ever wonder which bathroom to use—men's or women's—when you're in public? Or wonder what you're doing in the one you do eventually choose? Trans* individuals often don't have the privilege of *not* asking those questions. Trans* individuals have been harassed, beaten, and arrested for using the "wrong" bathroom (the one that belongs to their biological sex) as well as for using the "right" bathroom (the one that belongs to their gender presentation).

Safe bathrooms are an issue across the country, in many different settings. However, some communities are working on making sure restrooms are accessible and safe for everyone. Multnomah County, which includes the entire city of Portland, Oregon, is the first county in the nation to require single-stall gender-neutral restrooms in all new county-financed construction. The county is also exploring the possibility of retrofitting other public buildings with single-occupancy bathrooms. The Tigard-Tualatin School District in Washington County, Oregon, has also mandated at least one single-occupancy gender-neutral restroom in each of its middle and high school buildings.

At Grinnell College in Iowa, students in residence halls vote to determine whether the restrooms (and dorm rooms) on their floor will be gender neutral. Grinnell College also has a gender-neutral locker room. Private colleges such as Grinnell are more likely than public universities to have gender-neutral housing options, but the idea is growing in popularity.

Web developers have also taken steps to aid the search for safe bathrooms. The website safe2pee.org helps users find gender-neutral and single-stall bathrooms across the United States and in countries around the world.

For Natasha, the best relationship in her life is with Nancy: "She sees me for the person I am inside and loves me no matter what, and in return I love her immensely." Nancy loves Natasha just as much: "Zhe is who zhe is. I don't really look at her gender; instead I see her as a person whom I love for who she is, for her great personality. I love her no matter which gender she happens to be portraying at the time, so I tend to overlook that and see her for who she is." About her love for Natasha, Nancy adds, "I would have to say a lot of [my attraction] is her personality. She can be very sarcastic at times which, while occasionally being annoying, also reminds me of my father and therefore is endearing as well. She is also a bit of a nerd and helps me develop my inner nerd that had been lying dormant until I met her. Plus there is the benefit of how pretty she is, especially when she gets all dressed up."

TRANS* ONLINE

Being trans* in the twenty-first century is very different from being trans* at any other time in history. Individuals who are exploring their gender identity are able to build community in brand-new ways, thanks to online groups, websites, YouTube, and social media. Positive (and negative) first-person stories of surgery, hormones, transition, and everyday life as a trans* person help people feel less alone. A visual record of the trans* community also exists online. Photographers such as Mariette Pathy Allen and photography projects such as *Visible Bodies: Transgender Narratives Retold* provide glimpses into both virtual and real-life trans* communities. These new ways of building community have allowed trans* individuals to feel much less isolated than those who lived before the Internet became popular and widespread.

This sense of a larger community may be encouraging individuals to claim their trans* identities even earlier in their lives. Researchers Genny Beemyn and Sue Rankin discovered that more than two-thirds of the eighteen- to twenty-two-year-old respondents to their 2005–2006 survey knew someone who was trans* before they came out as trans* themselves. In contrast, only one-third of their interviewees in their forties and one-fourth of their interviewees in their fifties and older knew another trans* person prior to coming out. Beemyn and Rankin attribute these early community connections to the Internet.

With this larger awareness of trans* issues and trans* lives, the driver's license scenario that opened this book is likely to be very different in coming years. Someday a trans* individual may not have to worry about whether or not there's a box on the form that's appropriate for their gender identity. Someday the gender markers may include M(ale), F(female), and T(rans)—or gender markers may even become a thing of the past. No matter what, in the twenty-first century, Americans are understanding gender to be a much broader concept than ever before. Our lives are richer because of it.

This overview provides a brief look at key events in trans*gender history. Information about events before 1900 is included in the trans*history chapter. Check out the further information section on pages 84–86 to learn even more.

1907 The word *transsexual* is first used in print in the article "The Girl Who Travels Alone," published in the *Medical Times* journal in New York. Prior to the discovery of this reference, it was assumed that German physician Magnus Hirschfeld had first used the word (in German, *transsexualismus*) in 1923. Dr. Hirschfeld supervised some of the first genital reassignment surgeries ever done while he was on staff at the Institute for Sexual Science in Berlin. The institute was later destroyed by the Nazis in the 1930s, as part of a government censorship program.

1948 Dr. Harry Benjamin begins to use hormone therapy in the treatment of transsexual patients in San Francisco, California.

1952 Christine Jorgensen, an American World War II veteran, begins hormone therapy and gender reassignment surgery in Denmark. At this time, gender reassignment was available only in Europe. Born in 1926 as George William Jorgensen, she was the first person in the United States to receive any public attention for gender reassignment surgery. Her autobiography, *Christine Jorgensen: A Personal Biography*, was published in 1967. The book was turned into a film in 1970.

1966 The beginnings of trans* political resistance take shape in San Francisco's Tenderloin neighborhood. Unhappy with the behavior of a group of trans* youth patrons at Compton's Cafeteria, management calls the police. In response to rough treatment by the police, the trans* patrons resist and a riot ensues. The cafeteria declares that trans* patrons will no longer be admitted into the restaurant. Trans* patrons and their supporters picket the establishment in protest.

1969 Riots break out at the Stonewall Inn in New York City as the bar's gay patrons resist a police raid. The riot is considered the beginning of the modern gay rights movement. Trans* woman activist Sylvia Rivera was one of the leaders of the riot.

1972 Sweden becomes the first country in the world to legally allow a change in gender markers on official documents after gender reassignment surgery. However, Sweden requires all trans* individuals to be sterilized before undergoing the surgery. The sterilization law is repealed in 2013.

1977 Trans* woman and professional tennis player Renee Richards wins the right to play professional tennis as a woman after filing a lawsuit against the US Tennis Association.

1979 Researchers and medical doctors form the Harry Benjamin International Gender Dysphoria Association. (HBIGDA) to study and better understand gender dysphoria. Harry Benjamin was a German-born American physician widely known for his work with transsexuals from the 1940s onward. HBIGDA created standards of care for medical professionals in the treatment of trans* individuals. The most recent version of these standards was published in 2011 by the group, now called the World Professional Association for Transgender Health.

1984 GenderNet debuts as the first electronic bulletin board service (a precursor of the World Wide Web) for trans* individuals and their allies.

1993 Minnesota recognizes gender identity as a protected class with the passage of the state's Human Rights Act. It becomes the first state to ban employment discrimination based on gender identity.

Trans* man Brandon Teena is raped and murdered in Humboldt, Nebraska. The incident inspires the Academy Award–winning film *Boys Don't Cry* (1999).

1995 Georgina Beyer is elected the mayor of Carterton, on the North Island of New Zealand. She is the first trans* mayor in the world. She is later elected to New Zealand's parliament in 1999 and served until 2007.

1999 The first International Transgender Day of Remembrance is observed in memory of Rita Hester, an African American trans* woman who was murdered in 1998 in Massachusetts. The event continues worldwide every November 20 to honor those who have died from trans*-related violence.

2002 The Transgender Law Center is founded in San Francisco by young lawyers Dylan Vade (a trans* man) and Chris Daley, using money awarded from Echoing Green, a social justice foundation in New York. The center's stated mission is to work "to change law, policy, and attitudes so that all people can live safely, authentically, and free from discrimination regardless of their gender identity or expression." The center is the first of its kind.

2003 Trans* activist Mara Keisling founds the National Center for Transgender Equality, based in Washington, DC. The center is "dedicated to advancing the equality of transgender people through advocacy, collaboration, and empowerment."

2008 The television show *America's Next Top Model* features trans* woman Isis King as a contestant.

2009 President Barack Obama signs the Matthew Shepard and James Byrd Jr. Hate Crimes Prevention Act, which allows for federal investigation of bias-motivated crimes. Both men were murdered in 1998—Matthew Shepard (in Wyoming) because he was gay, and James Byrd Jr. (in Texas) because he was African American. Also in 2009, President Obama issues an executive order banning discrimination related to gender identity in employment decisions within the executive branch.

2010 President Obama appoints trans* woman Amanda Simpson as a senior technical adviser in the Department of Commerce's Bureau of Industry and Security.

2011 Anna Grodzka of Poland is elected to that nation's parliament, becoming the first trans* member of a European parliamentary body.

Basketball player Kye Allums becomes the first openly transgender athlete in the National Collegiate Athletic Association (NCAA).

Tom Léger and Riley MacLeod found Topside Press to publish "authentic transgender narratives."

2012 Canadian trans* woman Jenna Talackova wins her challenge to compete in the Miss Universe Canada pageant. The pageant had previously banned transgender contestants.

2013 Six-year-old trans* girl Coy Mathis wins the right to use bathrooms at her school that fit her gender identity rather than her assigned identity at birth. After the family filed a civil rights complaint, the Colorado Civil Rights Division ruled that the school district had violated the state's 2008 antidiscrimination statute.

The Netflix original series *Orange Is the New Black* debuts, featuring a trans* woman lead character named Sophia. Sophia is played by trans* woman Laverne Cox, making Sophia the first recurring trans* character in TV or film to be played by a trans* actor.

Students at Marina High School in Huntington Beach, California, choose Cassidy Campbell as their homecoming queen. She is the first openly trans* homecoming queen in the United States.

2014 Transgender student Nicole Maines of Orono, Maine, wins her court battle to use the bathroom in her school that fits her gender.

This list of prominent trans* Americans offers a glimpse into trans* contributions to the arts, politics, sports, and much more. It is not an exhaustive list, and readers are invited to research and learn more about other trans* individuals. Start by consulting the suggested further information section on pages 84–86. See how much you and your friends can grow the list!

TRANS*ARTS

Laura Jane Grace (b. 1980): Born Thomas Gabel and raised on army bases around the world, Laura Jane Grace is the lead singer of the Florida punk band Against Me! She decided to transition in May 2012, with the support of her wife, Heather.

RuPaul (b. 1960): RuPaul Andre Charles was born and raised in San Diego. He rose to fame as a drag performer and singer in New York. RuPaul hosts *RuPaul's Drag Race*, a reality drag show competition that launched in 2009 on the Logo channel.

Lana Wachowski (b. 1965): Born Lawrence Wachowski in Chicago, Illinois, Lana is a filmmaker, screenwriter, and producer. She has often worked with her younger brother, Andy, on projects such as *The Matrix* (1999) and *V for Vendetta* (2006). She began living as a woman in the 2000s.

TRANS*POLITICS

Kim Coco Iwamoto (b. 1968): An open trans* woman, Iwamoto is a commissioner on the Hawaii Civil Rights Commission, to which she was appointed in 2012. She had previously served on the Hawaii Board of Education. When she was elected to the Hawaii Board of Education in 2006, she became the highest-ranking trans* official in the United States and the first openly trans* person elected to a state office in Hawaii.

Stu Rasmussen (b. 1948): Raised in Silverton, Oregon, Rasmussen is the mayor of Silverton and the first openly transgender mayor in the United States.

Diego Sanchez (b. 1957): Born in Panama, Sanchez moved to Georgia at the age of seven. He is a former adviser to US representative Barney Frank (D-MA) and has served as the director of policy at PFLAG (Parents, Families, and Friends of Lesbians and Gays) since 2013.

TRANS*SPORTS

Fallon Fox (b. 1975): Born Boyd Burton in Toledo, Ohio, Fallon Fox competes in mixed martial arts matches. She underwent gender confirmation surgery in 2006, after serving four years in the US Navy.

Keelin Godsey (b. 1984): Born Kelly Godsey, he became the first openly transgender US Olympic candidate. He competed in tryouts as his assigned sex (female) and transitioned after his tryout. He now works as a physical therapist and coaches at a local college.

Gabrielle Ludwig (b. ca. 1961): Born Robert John Ludwig, Gabrielle started taking female hormones in 2007. After having sex reassignment surgery, she became the first transgender person to play college basketball as a male (in the 1980s) and as a female in 2012, when she began to play for Mission College's women's team at the age of fifty.

TRANS*PIONEERS

Kate Bornstein (b. 1948): An author, playwright, performance artist, and activist, Bornstein was raised in a conservative Jewish home. She later became a Scientologist but was excommunicated. She is best known for her books about trans* life and survival, and she is a frequent media commentator on trans* issues.

Leslie Feinberg (b. 1949): Feinberg is a writer, speaker, and activist. She is best known for applying elements of the labor rights movement to trans* rights work and is the author of *Transgender Warriors* and the groundbreaking trans* novel *Stone Butch Blues*.

Lou Sullivan (1951–1991): Born Sheila Jean Sullivan in Milwaukee, Wisconsin, Lou was an author and the founder of Female to Male (later FTM International), the first organization for female-to-male transsexuals. He was the first trans* man to die of AIDS. In 2007 the Lou Sullivan Society was formed to continue his work as a mentor and an advocate for trans* individuals.

TRANS*CELEBRITIES

Thomas Beatie (b. 1974): Born Tracy LaGondino in Honolulu, Hawaii, he gained notoriety as "the pregnant man." Having undergone a double mastectomy (but not a hysterectomy), he was still able to conceive and bear three children (from 2008 through 2010) through artificial insemination. He is a vocal advocate and public speaker for transgender fertility and reproductive rights.

Chaz Bono (b. 1969): Born Chastity Sun Bono to pop-star parents Sonny and Cher, Chaz is a trans* activist and writer who documented his transition in the 2011 book *Transition: Becoming Who I Was Always Meant to Be*. That same year, he also competed on *Dancing with the Stars*.

Carmen Carrera (b. 1985): Born Christopher Roman, Carrera competed on the third season of *RuPaul's Drag Race* as a man but transitioned after the show's season was over. A grassroots petition to make her a Victoria's Secret model was started in November 2013.

GLOSSARY

cisgender: an adjective that identifies an individual whose gender identity matches the sex assigned to the individual at birth. The prefix *cis* means "on the same side."

cross-dressing: wearing the clothes of the opposite gender. Cross-dressers used to be called transvestites. People usually cross-dress for comfort, pleasure, or public performance.

feminine: possessing or expressing characteristics and/or traits that are traditionally assigned to females

FTM (female to male): an older way of referring to a transsexual man

gender binary: classifying gender into two separate, distinct halves: male and female

gender confirmation surgery: surgical procedures that change a person's body to help it conform to a person's gender identity. The term for the surgery was once *sexual reassignment surgery*, or *SRS.*

gender dysphoria: the medical term (and the term used by insurance companies) for the condition in which a person's gender identity doesn't match the individual's assigned sex at birth. In previous decades, the term for this condition was *gender identity disorder.*

gender identity: a person's inner sense of being masculine, feminine, both, or neither

gender-neutral language: language that doesn't use traditional words such as *he*, *she*, *her*, or *him*, which are based in the male/female binary

gender-nonconforming: a label for someone whose gender expression and presentation is different from societal expectations for that gender

gender presentation/gender expression: a range of characteristics that tells us about an individual's gender identity. Gender expression and gender presentation can include clothes, behaviors, vocal characteristics, jobs, and activities.

genderqueer: a person who does not subscribe to traditional binary gender behaviors or appearances. That person may have a gender identity of neither male nor female or both or somewhere in between male and female.

gender spectrum: a range of gender expression that allows for flow between masculine and feminine characteristics or both or neither

hir: a gender-neutral pronoun used by some trans* individuals. The word is a combination of "his" and "her."

hormone therapy: the prescribed administration of estrogen or testosterone to help trans* individuals align their gender identities and their bodies

intersex: a physical condition in which a person has some combination of both female and male internal and/or external sexual organs. An individual who is intersex may also have a nontraditional combination of chromosomes instead of the traditional XX (female) or XY (male) pattern.

LGBT: a common acronym to indicate the lesbian, gay, bisexual, and transgender community. The acronym can also be written LGBTQ to include the queer community; LGBTQA to include the queer and ally communities; or LGBTQQIA to include the queer, questioning, intersex, and ally communities. The shorter acronym is sometimes written GLBT or GBLT.

masculine: possessing or expressing characteristics and/or traits that are traditionally assigned to males

MTF (male to female): an older way of referring to a transsexual woman

queer: the word usually indicates an open sexuality (outside the binary of gay/straight). It can also refer to an open or fluid gender presentation or to an open, liberal, and inclusive political stance toward LGBT issues.

sex chromosomes: the genetic markers in a human body that determine the features of human biological sex. Usually, the sex chromosomes of a female body are XX, and the sex chromosomes of a male body are XY.

sexual orientation: a term that expresses the gender configuration of a person's romantic and/or sexual partnerships (same-gender, opposite gender, etc.). Commonly recognized sexual orientations are lesbian, gay, straight, and bisexual.

they/their: in gender-neutral language, these plural pronouns are used in a singular manner to express the flexible gender identity of the person or people to whom they refer

trans*: in the computer world, an asterisk added to a search term asks the search to find all associations with that word. Added to the prefix *trans*, it refers to the many different gender identities associated with the term.

transfeminine: a term for a feminine identity chosen by a person assigned male at birth

transgender: an umbrella term for people whose gender expression or identity is different from the gender identity associated with their assigned sex at birth

transition: the period of time during which a person begins living as their preferred gender. Transitioning may include hormone therapy, gender confirmation surgery, a name change, or changes to legal documents to reflect the person's new gender.

transmasculine: a term for a masculine identity chosen by a person assigned female at birth

transsexual: a person whose gender identity is different from the individual's assigned sex at birth. Often transsexuals wish to alter their bodies with hormones or surgeries to make them more closely align with their gender identity.

trans (trans*) man: a transsexual person who was assigned a female identity at birth but now identifies as a male. A trans* man has usually had medical intervention to align his gender and biological identities. Another label for a trans* man is *FTM*.

trans (trans*) woman: a transsexual person who was assigned a male identity at birth but now identifies as a female. A trans* woman has usually had medical intervention to align her gender and biological identities. Another label for a trans* woman might be *MTF*.

zhe: a gender-neutral personal pronoun used by some trans* individuals as a combination of "he" and "she"

9 Hayden Northup, e-mail interview with the author, November 28, 2012.

10 Ibid.

10 Ibid.

10 Karlee Holets, e-mail interview with the author, November 28, 2012.

11 Ibid.

11 Ibid.

11–12 Diana Dohmen, e-mail interview with the author, November 28, 2012.

12 Ibid.

12 Ibid.

12 Hayden Northup, e-mail interview with the author, November 28, 2012.

14 Adriana Garibay e-mail interview with the author, January 8, 2014.

29 Dean Kotula, e-mail interview with the author, January 21, 2013.

29 Ibid.

29 Ibid.

29 Ibid.

30 Ibid.

30 Ibid.

30 Ibid.

31 Ibid.

31 Ibid.

31 Ibid.

31–32 Ibid.

33 Ibid.

33 Ibid.

33 Ibid.

19 Katie Burgess, e-mail interview with the author, November 9, 2012.

19–20 Ibid.

20 Ibid.

20 Ibid.

20 Ibid.

20 Ibid.

20 Ibid.

21 Ibid.

21 Ibid.

21 Ibid.

21–22 Ibid.

23 Ibid.

35 David Gaer, e-mail interview with the author, October 28, 2012.

35 Ibid.

36 Ibid.

36 Ibid.

36–37 Ibid.

37 Ibid.

45 Jaime FlorCruz, "Jin Xing: China's Sex-Change Pioneer," *CNN.com*, July 11, 2013, http://www.cnn.com/2013/07/11/world/asia/china-jin-xing-sex-change/.

47 Brooke Wilcoxson, FaceTime interview with the author, March 28, 2013.

48 Ibid.

48 Ibid.

49 Ibid.

49 Ibid.

49 Ibid.

49 Ibid.

50 Ibid.

50 Ibid.

53 Cary Gabriel Costello, "On Trans* People and Suicide," *TransFusion* (blog), April 14, 2013, http://trans-fusion.blogspot.com/2013/04/on-trans-people-and-suicide.html.

57 Julia Keleher, e-mail interview with the author, September 12, 2012.

57 Ibid.

57–58 Ibid.

58 Ibid.

58 Ibid.

58 Ibid.

58 Ibid.

59 Ibid.

62 American Civil Liberties Union (ACLU) Lesbian Gay Bisexual Transgender & AIDS Project, "Know Your Rights—Transgender People and the Law," April 24, 2013, https://www.aclu.org/lgbt-rights/know-your-rights-transgender-people-and-law.

63 GLAAD (Gay & Lesbian Alliance Against Defamation), "Transgender Day of Remembrance #TDOR—November 20," GLAAD.com, accessed November 14, 2013, http://www.glaad.org/tdor.

64 CeCe McDonald, "A Major Milestone: My 25th Birthday!," *Support CeCe McDonald!* (blog), May 17, 2013, http://supportcece.wordpress.com/category/ceces-blog/.

67 Natasha Rosenberg, e-mail interview with the author, November 13, 2012.

67 Ibid.

67 Ibid.

67 Ibid.

68 Ibid.

68 Nancy Bebernes, e-mail interview with the author, November 13, 2012.

68 Rosenberg, interview.

68 Ibid.

70 Ibid.

70 Bebernes, interview.

70 Ibid.

Beemyn, Genny, and Susan Rankin. *The Lives of Transgender People.* New York: Columbia University Press, 2011.

Eells, Josh, "The Secret Life of Tom Gabel." *Rolling Stone,* no. 1157 (May 24, 2012): 54–60.

Feinberg, Leslie. *Transgender Warriors.* Boston: Beacon Press, 1996.

Girshick, Lori B. *Transgender Voices: Beyond Women and Men.* Hanover, NH: University Press of New England, 2008.

Grant, Jaime M., Lisa A. Mottet, Justin Tanis, Jack Harrison, Jody L. Herman, and Mara Keisling. *Injustice at Every Turn: A Report of the National Transgender Discrimination Survey.* Washington, DC: National Center for Transgender Equality and the National Gay and Lesbian Task Force, 2011. Accessed November 14, 2013. http://www. thetaskforce.org/reports_and_research/ntds.

Grant, Jaime M., Lisa A. Mottet, Justin Tanis, Jody L. Herman, Jack Harrison, and Mara Keisling. *National Transgender Discrimination Survey Report on Health and Health Care: Findings of a Study by the National Center for Transgender Equality and the National Gay and Lesbian Task Force.* Washington, DC: National Center for Transgender Equality and the National Gay and Lesbian Task Force, 2010. Accessed November 14, 2013. http://www.ngltf.org/reports_and_research/trans_survey_health_heathcare.

PBS. "Two Spirits: A Map of Gender-Diverse Cultures." *Independent Lens.* May 20, 2011. http://www.pbs.org/independentlens/two-spirits/map.html.

Stryker, Susan. *Transgender History.* Berkeley, CA: Seal Press, 2007.

Torre, Pablo S., and David Epstein. "The Transgender Athlete." *Sports Illustrated* 116, no. 22 (May 28, 2012): 66–73.

Townsend, Megan. "Timeline: A Look Back at the History of Transgender Visibility." GLAAD.org. November 19, 2012. http://www.glaad.org/blog/timeline-look-back-history-transgender-visibility.

"Transgender." *Wikipedia.* June 13, 2013. http://en.wikipedia.org/wiki/Transgender.

"The Trans Timeline." *Trans History.* Accessed December 1, 2013. http://tghistory.org/.

FOR FURTHER INFORMATION

FICTION

Beam, Cris. *I Am J*. New York: Little, Brown Books for Young Readers, 2011.

Brezenoff, Steve. *Brooklyn Burning*. Minneapolis: Carolrhoda Lab, 2011.

Cronn-Mills, Kirstin. *Beautiful Music for Ugly Children*. Woodbury, MN: Flux, 2012.

Davis, Tanita. *Happy Families*. New York: Knopf Books for Young Readers, 2012.

Gold, Rachel. *Being Emily*. Tallahassee, FL: Bella Books, 2012.

Hyde, Catherine Ryan. *Jumpstart the World*. Fort Walton Beach, FL: Ember Press, 2011.

Katcher, Bryan. *Almost Perfect*. New York: Delacorte, 2009.

Peters, Julie Anne. *Luna*. New York: Little, Brown Books for Young Readers, 2003.

Wittlinger, Ellen. *Parrotfish*. New York: Simon & Schuster Books for Young Readers, 2012.

NONFICTION

Amato, Toni, and Mary Davies, eds. *Pinned Down by Pronouns*. Jamaica Plain, MA: Conviction Books, 2003.

Beam, Cris. *Transparent: Love, Family, and Living the T with Transgender Teenagers*. Boston: Mariner Books, 2008.

Beck, Kristin. With Anne Spechkard. *Warrior Princess: A U.S. Navy SEAL's Journey to Coming Out Transgender*. McLean, VA: Advances Press, 2013.

Bono, Chaz. *Transition: Becoming Who I Was Always Meant to Be*. New York: Dutton, 2011.

Bornstein, Kate. *Gender Outlaws: The Next Generation*. Berkeley, CA: Seal Press, 2010.

————. *Hello, Cruel World: 101 Alternatives to Suicide for Teens, Freaks, and Other Outlaws*. New York: Seven Stories Press, 2006.

————. *My New Gender Workbook*, 2nd ed. London: Routledge, 2013.

Boylan, Jennifer Finney. *She's Not There*. New York: Broadway Books, 2003.

Kotula, Dean. *The Phallus Palace*. Boston: Alyson Books, 2002.

Kuklin, Susan. *Beyond Magenta: Transgender Teens Speak Out*. Somerville, MA: Candlewick, 2014.

WEBSITES

Intersex Society of North America
> http://www.isna.org/
> The society's mission is "devoted to systemic change to end shame, secrecy, and unwanted genital surgeries for people born with an anatomy that someone decided is not standard for male or female." The website is a great resource for information about intersex conditions, including resources regarding medical and legal issues.

MiMi Van Dorn
> https://www.facebook.com/groups/594122540666777/
> This Facebook page spotlights MiMi Van Dorn, the drag queen persona of Dave Gaer, who is profiled in this book.

National Center for Transgender Equality
> http://www.transequality.org/
> The center is "dedicated to advancing the equality of transgender people through advocacy, collaboration, and empowerment." The website offers resources for trans* individuals ranging from information about legal rights to military benefits for veterans. This website is one of the most respected trans* websites on the Internet.

The Sylvia Rivera Law Project
> http://srlp.org/
> The Silvia Rivera Law Project offers legal services to trans* and queer individuals as well as training to allies. The project also offers information to build grassroots advocacy and fund-raising campaigns to support trans* causes.

Transgender and Gender Identity Respect Campaign
> http://ohr.dc.gov/transrespect
> This civil rights ad campaign appeared citywide in bus shelters and online in Washington, DC, during the fall and winter of 2012. The images featured a photo and mini profile of five different gender-nonconforming citizens of the nation's capital.

Transgender Law Project
> http://transgenderlawcenter.org/
> The Transgender Law Center works "to change law, policy, and attitudes so that all people can live safely, authentically, and free from discrimination regardless of their gender identity or expression." The website offers information about identity documents and family, health-care, and many other legal topics.

World Professional Association for Transgender Health
> http://www.wpath.org/
> This organization (and website) provides information to consumers as well as to medical professionals regarding scientific conferences about trans* medical issues. The site also provides a professional standards of care document that medical professionals can follow when treating transsexual individuals.

FILM AND TV

Beautiful Boxer (Thailand). 2003. This biographical sports film provides the life story of *kathoey* kickboxer Nong Toom (Nong Thoom).

Boys Don't Cry. 1999. This Academy Award–winning film explores the story behind the real-life 1993 murder of Brandon Teena, a trans* man in Nebraska. Teena is played by Hilary Swank.

Ma Vie En Rose (My Life in Pink) (Belgium). 1997. This Golden Globe–winning film follows young Ludovic (assigned male at birth) as she grows up insisting she is a girl to her unbelieving family and friends.

Normal. 2003. This Emmy- and Golden Globe–nominated television film explores how a family transitions along with its patriarch, Roy, when he comes out as a trans* woman on the twenty-fifth anniversary of his wedding.

Southern Comfort. 2001. This award-winning documentary tracks the last year in the life of Robert Eads, a trans* man who died from cancer in 1999 because of medical discrimination.

Transgeneration. 2005. This award-winning, eight-episode Sundance Channel documentary follows four trans* teens during one year of their college lives.

Two Spirits. 2011. This award-winning PBS television documentary explores the history of two-spirit individuals in indigenous American cultures through the story of a mother's loss of her two-spirit son.

INDEX

ABOUT THE AUTHOR

Kirstin Cronn-Mills, PhD, teaches writing, literature, and critical thinking classes at
South Central College in North Mankato, Minnesota. She writes fiction, poetry, and
nonfiction books and articles. Her young adult novels include the Minnesota Book Award
finalist *The Sky Always Hears Me and the Hills Don't Mind* and the Lambda Literary Award
finalist *Beautiful Music for Ugly Children*, winner of the 2014 American Library Association's
Stonewall Book Award. *Beautiful Music* follows Gabe, a trans* music geek, in a poignant
coming-of-age story.